thunder & lightning

thunder & lightning

TEAYUH

Copyright © 2020 by teayuh
All rights reserved, including the right to
reproduce, distribute, or transmit in any form or
by any means.

Edited by teayuh and Christian Torres
Cover design by Jay Orcutt
Photography by Jay Orcutt

ISBN 979-8-61636-643-6

Manufactured in the United States of America

Second Edition January 2024

Dedicated to my beloved cats and best friends, Thunder and Lightning.

Rest in peace, Thunder.
2/28/19

|from the author|

The Purest Form of Love
by *teayuh*

    I was eight years old when I fell in love for the first time. My earliest memory was our meeting. She was quiet, existing and present. Initially, I was the one to communicate, and within the following months she blossomed. We hardly spent any time apart.

    When night came, I'd see her in my dreams. She knew my greatest fears and hopes, as much as a young child could. As I aged, she wasn't far behind. Soon, I wasn't eight anymore but in my late teens. She still stood by me.

    My peers and community would repeatedly try to separate us and diminish our bond. It eventually caused our relationship to stumble and we reached a breaking point. I was 27 then, clutching at my chest in hysterics. It seemed we were going to fail. Darkness attempted to envelop me and hide her light. She cradled me until I fell asleep and dreamt of her.

41 greeted me like a stranger. I was compelled to look back by people who I thought were my friends. They showed me how much I had seemingly missed and were quick to point to her as the cause. Familiar with those types of actions, I turned them away and embraced her. Of course, we had been through everything together. She beamed with pride at my college graduation and cried tears of joy when I received my first promotion in my career. We even shared a house, though she made it a home.

Now, at 75, I sense we are fading. Older now, and wiser, our physical weaknesses are closing in, yet we have never been stronger. All these years we've been partners. I sank into her loyalty and reflected just the same.

I was eight years old when I fell in love for the first time. As I grew, people tried to tear me down and persuade me to despise who I saw looking back at me. I never bowed for their satisfaction… and she reveled with me in victory.

While we may be nearing the end, I find comfort knowing my journey was wonderful. I always have my hand to hold. She squeezes back in reassurance.

thunder & lightning

more

Perhaps love isn't what we thought it was

Perhaps it's more...

more than a balance of joy and heartache

more than a balance of warmth and the cold

Maybe it's more than guilt from wrong doing

and the rush of a kiss

a tender touch

Yes, it's more than butterflies in our stomachs

it's more than a shared laugh

more than a shared understanding

Love is more than the tears we shed

and the meaningful embraces

It's more than compassion, safety, pain, loyalty and trust..

Love is more
It's just more

buddha

You can call it weakness,
as if I've never heard it

You can call it shame,
as if I've never felt it

You can push me outside your limits while
your eyes never leave hands,
but these wrinkled cheeks are still a path for
sorrow

It would be cowardly of me to deny my
emotions

You could only wish to show yourself such
devotion

sun bathing

They say freedom is with the wind,
running through hair with childlike wonder

I've found it is the sun
This life breathing star we've always been under

She touches our skin and warms our bones
She sends her love so we can build our homes

She brightens our future
and stretches her rays
to ensure we are safe
from night until day

With her, you are weightless
With her, you are clean

Embrace her affection

glazed

An object of affection
Oh, how dangerous it can be

Seen as the ultimate goal
To share this life

The good outweighs the bad

An object of affection
Oh, how dangerous it can be

The memories you'll make…
and the stories you'll tell

An object of affection
Oh, how dangerous it can be

To put your soul into a camera battery

Just look at the pictures

They had all of my affection
Oh, how painful it can be

Life without them is obscure
I never thought to buy a charger

if you could see me now

If you could see me now,
I hope you'd be proud

I hope you'd wrap me in your energy and
never let this go

If you could see me now,
I hope I'd make you laugh

I've honestly begun to see the humor in
spilled milk

If you could see me now,
I hope we'd dance

I know I told you it wasn't my thing,
but my ears and my feet have settled their
differences

If you could see me now,
I hope you'd understand

I didn't mean any of it

If you could see me now,
and I could look into your eyes,
I'd never look away again

nowhere to go

Nowhere to go
Nowhere to run

I don't know how to get away from myself

My chest is on fire but
my eyes burn the most

My mouth is dry but
my eyelashes are soaked

I want to give it all to you
I want you to feel my love

As time continues on
It just builds and builds

With nowhere to go
I fall apart

loss

In reality,
you can't lose something you never had

If you had it,
why'd you let it go?

If you didn't let it go,
why didn't I appreciate them more?

If I did appreciate them,
why didn't I tell them I loved them?

And if I loved them,
why aren't they here?

Isn't love supposed to be enough?
Or is loss stronger?

deep breaths

I can't tell my five senses apart
as I lay on my side with your hand on my
shoulder

"What time is it?" I ask
"Focus on me" You say

I think I'm starving
The seasons are changing too quickly

"How long have we been here?" I ask
"Take a deep breath" You say

Function can be exasperating after losing all
reasons to

be there

Another day is never promised

As long as we have been here,
we've been moving

Moving together
and moving apart

Before another day passes,
let's just be here

Let's just be here and enjoy this

the recharge

Lay in bed and watch the clock
Watch without any weight
Let yourself be light when resting

I know you've been here awhile
Have patience with yourself
It's the absence you're still digesting

There will be times you reach for them
It is okay to come up empty
And to find trouble with accepting

Though the world will not stop
Know they'd want better for you
So let yourself be light when resting

never imagined

How short it could be
or how sharp
The constant sting of a paper cut
across your heart
Growing up, they told you
"Be prepared from the start"
Love heals all things
and can still tear you apart

on hold

I tried calling you yesterday
Voicemail, again
It's alright, I'm used to it now

She's gotten so big since you last saw her
Her first day of school went great
and I've managed to get by somehow

I know you can't talk
but I know you can still listen
Darling, I'm counting the days

When I see you again
I'll have even more to share
and probably less to say

inside and out

Inside
I'm hollow

                                      Outside
                                    I'm playful

Inside
I echo

                                      Outside
                                    I'm solid

Inside
I'm hungry and nauseous

                                      Outside
                      I carry purpose in my stride

Inside
I'm static

                                      Outside
                                  I'm motivated

Inside
I'm fragile

                                      Outside
                                  I'm moving

Inside
I'm wary and cautious

                                      Outside
                         I'm beaming with pride

Inside
I'm a million degrees
I'm frozen

> Outside
> I'm open
> I'm courageous and outspoken

Inside
I'm wailing
I'm screaming
I'm broken

> Outside
> I show no true emotions

human

If they've never been through it
send them pity
Because sooner or later,
they'll need it

an order

You can still be your own sergeant
Your own chief
Your own captain

You can still be your own director
Your own boss
Your own leader

But having personal time off is needed

beef jerky

When you look back
to find peace
When you look back
to find joy in the memories,
understand they don't have to be big
or expensive
or widely known

The best come from the small,
from the private,
and from the heart

level with me

Please don't hide from me
You aren't a burden
Please don't shut me out
I'm here if you need someone

Please don't lie to me
I can see the dried tears on your cheeks
Please don't be ashamed
It's okay to show vulnerability

things i wanted to say

You are the best friend I've ever had

I love that you never judge me for being myself

Your constant support in everything I do makes me work harder

I've never laughed with someone as much as I've laughed with you

Your presence in my life makes me a better person

When I wake up, I think of you

Before I fall asleep, I think of you

When I'm asleep, I dream of you

I love myself when I'm around you

I love you

remote control

If life were really like a movie,
and I had the remote control…

If life were really like a movie,
and I had the power…

If life were really like a movie,
I'd constantly hit rewind

I could see you again
and hold you in my arms

I could take in your sweet scent
and watch your smile light up a room
like it lit up my life

I could listen to you laugh
and joke around with you for hours

If life were really like a movie,
I wouldn't need to hit rewind
because you'd still be here

common

I've been where you are now
It may not be under the same circumstances
but I know those emotions

I know that ear splitting cry
I know the numbness in your limbs
and the weight that punches you repeatedly
in the chest

I know how your throat becomes tight and
feels like it's closing so all you're able to let
out is a hoarse sob

I know how your heart beats against your
ear drums
and how your vision blurs out the world

I know that your insides are pulling against
each other and you want to get sick,
hoping it'll make it all stop

I know it all too well
So do others

Misplacing your anger
your heartbreak
and pushing it onto them

It's not going to help

So if they offer their shoulder,
try leaning

Until you can see again
Until you're able to speak
Until you're able to hold yourself up

They will be patient as long as you let them

photogenic

I see your pictures now

I wish I had captured every moment with you

I wish you hadn't convinced me to delete the ones you didn't like

I wish you would've believed me when I told you that you were beautiful

You always said I was just being modest

end of day

Throughout the day,
I am numb
I struggle with acceptance

Throughout the day,
I am angry
at the truth of your absence

Throughout the day,
I flinch
because with every passing moment
I see your face

Throughout the day,
I am hatred
because I know it's something that can't be erased

At the end of the day,
I'm a little more prepared for tomorrow

transformation

The scars you collect will shed
and your new skin will be much thicker
Much stronger than before
So you'll be better prepared the next time
death comes knocking at your door

forgiveness

A time of grieving
You're thrust into a downward spiral
Keep steady
and remember to be gentle with yourself

flying saucer

They say to feel someone
beyond touch
is as real as the Loch Ness Monster

They say to see someone
beyond the grave
is as real as a flying saucer

Love is limitless,
even in reality

grounding

You can want to be enraged
You can want revenge
You can want pain
You can even want longing,
justice,
and someone to blame

You can want everything and nothing
Yet, with you, I plead
Focus less on the want
and more on the need

believe me or not

I've been where you are
I was stuck for days,
weeks,
months even
Uninterested in my passions
and to shower took too much motivation

I pushed away the ones that were still here
I talked less
I slept more
Crying became tiresome

I've been where you are
but I'm here now

Believe me or not,
it gets better

healing

Trying to put the pieces back together
isn't selfish
Working towards a future is part of it

we are lucky

We gave our hearts to someone
who opened our souls tenfold

We held hands with someone
whose presence became our home

We sacrificed for someone
whose growth made us glow

We loved unconditionally
and they'll never know

they

Lifted you up,
spun you around,
gave you the confidence
for your feet to touch the ground

Hold still
Stay balanced
Don't fall on them now

Make them root for you
in your dreams
You're going to make them proud

noodle arms

"I don't remember how." You say,
looking down at the floor

"It's alright. Trust in me." She says,
"I've done this before."

She guides your arms up
and around,
holding you close

An embrace you had forgotten
but needed the most

but the kitchen sink

A minor inconvenience
into a tidal wave of waterworks

A small disagreement
into a full out brawl

A joke only a father could be proud of
into a fit of laughter

One hundred times
One thousand times
Everything but the kitchen sink

… and then some

come back

I want to see the light in your eyes
and I demand you take back our goodbyes
When I wake in the morning
I need you to be there

Please, someone,
anyone,
make this right
because it's just not fair

masks

They mourn them
like they knew them
Knew what made their spirit soar
Knew the last thought to run through their
mind
And as you witness their
best performance yet,
you don't feel anger
or rage
Instead, you are filled with content
in knowing you were lucky enough

horoscope

Months pass
Seasons too
There is always new life to categorize

Our bond is one thing
that could not be determined
no matter how hard they tried

dehydrated

The pounding in my head
Tongue like sandpaper
Energy as low as the ground
I never thought I could miss motivation
as much as I do now
You were so refreshing

lately

I've been thinking of you
and our late night car rides
Convincing my grandfather to get us food
and laughing until we couldn't breathe

We didn't part how I wanted
In fact, I never thought we would
But life has a funny way of happening
Lately, I've been thinking of you
and I hope you're well

marco polo

Drowning, at first
The hit took everything from my lungs
Panic set in
Then, I heard your voice
and started to rise
When I reached the surface
I stayed floating
You were nowhere in sight
I know I heard you
I'm always feeling you
It's become my favorite game

unspoken

You don't have to know what to feel
No one can decide for you
You feel something under the numbness
That's more than enough

rose garden

She never was a fan of receiving flowers
"They'll die, anyways"

Every afternoon,
she waters the garden

Now her mother, on the other hand,
her favorite were roses

thunder and lightning

I am a gift
                                      I come with life
I am unexpected
                                          As am I
I make your heart skip
                And I make it stop completely
I can bring you to your knees
                            I can make you stronger
I help you create memories
          And I make you look back on them
People search for me
                            I am what they try to avoid
I build
                                            I break
Many believe
                            we are enemies
If you look closer
                              you will see
we are one   we are one
                in the same

when one door closes

The vexation I feel when given instruction,
not advice,
on how to deal with heartbreak
is indescribable

No one ever considers that my room is on fire
All exits are blocked
even though they are open

like a raven

As mighty as an eagle
As passionate as a dove
As fierce as a hawk
As graceful as a hummingbird

Prey and beauty
Respected and admired
by many

Oh, to be like a raven,
my chosen familiar
It has to be the strongest
to deal with such darkness

blinding

You will never fully prepare yourself
No matter how many warning signs
you read

You will never fully prepare yourself
No matter how many words of
encouragement you breathe

You will never fully prepare yourself
No matter how many fists you make

You will never fully prepare yourself
No matter how many videos you take

You will never fully prepare yourself
With your hair disheveled and your teeth
grinding

You will never fully prepare yourself
Time will stop and the picture will be
blinding

always with you

I look down upon you
My heart swells
You've grown so much

I sit beside you when you come to visit
Your laugh is still the same
Music to my ears

I see the way you look at her
You used to look at me
I approve

I imagine the touch of your skin
against mine once more
We belonged to one another

I dream with you when you're asleep
so I can know what's going on in that head
Obviously, can't ask you directly

I cried when your dad passed
and your mom broke down in your arms
You were too strong to shed a tear

I listen when you argue with her
Still have the same stubborn mindset
It drives us both mad

I smile when she puts you in your place
It's about time someone did
You can't get your two cents in every time

I fear you're still hesitating
You know she's breaking down that wall
you spent years building
Don't be afraid

I know you still love me
I still love you
That's why I'm always around

I send you these thoughts
Each day, you get closer to moving on
Rooting from the sidelines

my treasure

I wanted to put you in my shirt pocket
and then our heartbeats would naturally
align

I wanted to lock you in a room with me
take the key
and toss it
and lay with you until the sun began to shine

I wanted to bury you in the sand
and possess the only copy of the map

I wanted so much of you,
with you,
and still
no one told me that love could be a trap

over the rainbow

My darling
We never saw one another
but you were the most beautiful soul I ever
laid eyes on

To know you was to love unconditionally

I dream of you often,
especially when I'm awake
It's easier to function this way

I think you'd have my sense of humor
and your mother's drive
Gosh, she was so strong for you

Thank you for what we have now
I can't wait to meet you
and dance in your colors

whiskers

There was little he could say or do
besides be there
It was always enough

In the middle of the night,
when his human was too drained to move about,
he moved closer
Close enough to brush his whiskers
against their nose

That faint tickle was reassurance
It was friendship
It was the freedom to go off at any time but
choosing to stay through the worst

It was all just a memory now
A painful, wonderful memory

gandhi

Patience
Seeking solace
Grasping for control over time

Do not waste yourself with attempts at a forceful change
Use that energy to step back
and let it do what it will

something sour

Let them pull away if they want to
Let them break down if they need to

Let them lean against you when they
become off balanced

When they look back on this
they will see something sweet,
finding content in what they thought would
be nothing but sour memories

Don't be something sour

to the moon and back

My love for you can travel any distance

It can fly to the moon
We'll be rendered weightless
with no gravity to hold us down

It can wrap around the sun,
pulling her up during an overcast
Her rays can surpass any and every obstacle

It can lick the stars
Their stardust will fall upon our heads
We will be blessed for all eternity

I love you to the moon and back
Are you ready to take this journey with me?

sunflower

When I see a sunflower
I can't help but smile

Such a large and tall flower,
with a stem as thick as a thumb,
fully grown yet still reaching towards her
mother

She is golden on sunny days
and yellow when it is raining
She never glooms with her surroundings
until it's time for her to go
and come around next year

When I see her
I can't help but smile

basket case

The first few months are the hardest
Seemingly hopeless and never ending
You fall out of love with the world
You may even fall out of love with yourself

rachel

It's been almost six years without you
I'd be lying if I said I thought about you
every day
I've never forgotten, though
You know I never will

You're the reason I say "I love you"
every time I leave the house,
no matter the circumstance
Sometimes I feel like I'm saying it for you
because you didn't get the chance

iced coffee

So he likes hiking when it rains?
Go with him

So she likes iced coffee in the winter?
Ask her to order two

So they enjoy dancing with no music?
Hum them a beat

Don't take someone's happiness because it's the opposite of yours

the casino

Can't be bent in your favor
The chips will fall where they may
Everyone is guaranteed an experience
the moment they walk through those doors
It's a gamble
It's a game
Enjoy the ride

clairvoyant

They'll see what they want to
and beg for forgiveness afterwards
You'll see what you need to
and come home to silence
Quality over quantity

send you an invitation

Our scrapbook of memories no longer holds
the infinite that we had hoped together
My eyes water when thinking of how many
moments you'll miss with me

I know you won't come but…
I'll still send you an invitation

twist my arm

Don't apologize to me
because I know it's a habit
Ask me
I'm open to you
Twist my arm
I'm flexible
Please don't apologize to me

what i really regret

I'm told I regret not being able to say
goodbye
I'm told I regret not taking enough time
I'm told I regret not answering that phone
call
What I really regret is not appreciating
having you in my life
If I had,
they wouldn't tell me anything

after the storm

It will be quiet as the water settles into the ground
All will hesitate before coming out from their hiding spots

You've seen it before
but never like this

It's a calm feeling
It is the acceptance of what happened

And so life keeps moving

thunder & lightning

| Meet The Author |

teayuh is a small town native of western Massachusetts. She found a love for poetry at seven years old and has been writing ever since, whether it be to pass the time or to share with the world. *teayuh* has always found it easier to express her thoughts and feelings through writing and considers writing her <u>safe place</u>. She always hopes that her work helps others to realize that they are not alone in their emotions.

When she isn't writing, *teayuh* can be found taking naps, cuddling with her cats, watching movies, reading, longboarding, or drinking unhealthy amounts of iced tea.

thunder & lightning

TEAYUH

Made in the USA
Middletown, DE
29 July 2024